PRAISE FOR
THE BITE-SIZED ENTREPRENEUR

"Got 5 minutes while waiting for a phone call? Instead of checking email -- again -- take a bite of The Bite-Sized Entrepreneur. *You'll find plenty of tips to stay motivated and productive, and build your business while building your life."*

--Laura Vanderkam, author of Off The Clock: Feel Less Busy While Getting More Done

"You can create the life you imagined and still be an entrepreneur. Damon's new book will give you the easy way to implement strategies and do just that. Entrepreneurship is the best gig ever only if you do it the way Damon lays out. Otherwise, you'll be working for the worst boss you ever had."

--Cameron Herold, author of Double Double *and* Meetings Suck

"In The Ultimate Bite-Sized Entrepreneur, *Damon Brown proves that you don't need to don a hoodie, move to Silicon Valley and sacrifice all your sleep (and sanity) to make it in the world of self-employment. Through his road-tested wisdom and interviews with successful innovators who have built businesses on their own terms, Damon provides practical, tactical advice to grow your business one small, delicious, perfectly bite-sized step at a time."*
--*Jenny Blake, author of* Pivot: The Only Move That Matters Is Your Next One

"Damon has filled this book with bite sized advice on both the mindset and actions required to have a thriving creative career. It's one of those books that you'll keep on your desk and frequently refer back to."

--*Srinivas Rao, author of* Unmistakable: Why Only Is Better Than Best

"For every would-be entrepreneur who's wondered if it's possible to "crush it" without crushing yourself, this book is for you! In this concise read, Inc. columnist Damon Brown lays out a road map for launching a satisfying and successful business without overturning the life you currently have."
–Meagan Francis, founder, the Life, Listened podcast network

"Sure, it starts with passion, but what do you know about living the life of an entrepreneur? The Bite-Sized Entrepreneur *gives smart, succinct advice about how to follow your business dreams, including why to treat Tuesday like Monday; the difference between busyness and productivity; and three effective ways of saying 'no.' Highly recommended for would-be entrepreneurs and freelancers."*
--Kelly K. James, author of Six-Figure Freelancing, Second Edition: The Writer's Guide to Make More Money

"A practical and actionable guide to accomplishing your goals that can help anyone master the mindset needed to become a self-made success."
—Scott Steinberg, bestselling author of Make Change Work for You

"In The Bite-Sized Entrepreneur, Damon Brown lays waste to both the misconceptions and pesky little lies we tell ourselves about why we can't make our side hustles a reality. A thoughtful, provocative read, Brown will help you understand why you have more time than you think to follow your passions—and offers smart, actionable advice to help you implement the right strategies so you can make your side hustle successful within the boundaries of the life you live today."
—Kayt Sukel, author of The Art of Risk and This Is Your Brain On Sex

THE BALANCED BITE-SIZED ENTREPRENEUR

BITE-SIZED ENTREPRENEUR BOOK #3
18 BUSINESS TACTICS TO HARMONIZE YOUR LIFE, LOVE & PURPOSE

Damon Brown
Inc.com columnist &
Co-Founder of Cuddlr
www.JoinDamon.me

PUBLISHED BY:
Damon Brown

The Bite-Sized Entrepreneur, 1st Edition
Copyright 2017 by Damon Brown
Edited by Jeanette Hurt
Cover designed by Bec Loss

Some material has been graciously reprinted or inspired by my work on Inc. Magazine Online, within random tweets, and on scribbled index cards. Thank you.

All rights reserved. Without limiting the rights under copyright reserved above, no part of this publication may be reproduced, stored in or introduced into a retrieval system, or transmitted, in any form, or by any means (electronic, mechanical, photocopying, recording, or otherwise) without the prior written permission of both the copyright owner and the above publisher of the book.

The author acknowledges the trademarked status and trademark owners of various products referenced in this work, which have been used without permission. The publication/use of these trademarks is not authorized, associated with, or sponsored by the trademark owners.

*To Parul,
my partner on this wild, wonderful journey.
Thank you.*

x

"Everybody is trying to do their best, and sometimes they don't even know it."

- Phil Jackson, Oprah's Super Soul Conversations

READING

THE BITE-SIZED

ENTREPRENEUR SERIES — XVIII

SELECTED BOOKS BY THE AUTHOR — XIX

WHY THIS BOOK SHOULDN'T EXIST — 1

18 STRATEGIES

I: LET GO

1. THE 3-MINUTE RULE — 9
2. YOU NEED LONGER DEADLINES — 15
3. PUT YOUR MASK ON FIRST — 19
4. CHECK THE WEATHER — 21
5. FAILURE CAN BE SUCCESS — 25
6. DO GOOD ENOUGH — 29
7. KNOW YOUR SACRIFICE — 35

8.	THE ULTIMATE TIME LIMIT	39
9.	THE BIGGEST CHANGES	43

II: Take In

10.	EVERY SINGLE DAY	49
11.	CARRY ONE THING AT A TIME	53
12.	BUILD LIKE YOU'RE ALREADY THERE	57
13.	THE 20/20 TECHINQUE	61
14.	THEORY IS JUST THAT	65
15.	DOING THEIR BEST	69
16.	IT ISN'T YOUR MONEY	73
17.	YOU'RE ALREADY SUCCESSFUL	79
18.	MIND THE GAP	83

LET'S CONNECT!	85
AVAILABLE KEYNOTE TALKS	87

FIVE MORE GREAT BOOKS TO READ   91

SIGNIFICANT QUOTES & REFERENCES   95

ACKNOWLEDGEMENTS   101

ABOUT THE AUTHOR   107

THE BITE-SIZED ENTREPRENEUR SERIES

THE ULTIMATE BITE-SIZED ENTREPRENEUR

TRILOGY:

76 WAYS TO BOOST TIME, PRODUCTIVITY & FOCUS

ON YOUR BIG IDEA

(KINDLE, PAPERBACK, AUDIOBOOK)

THE BITE-SIZED ENTREPRENEUR:

21 WAYS TO IGNITE YOUR PASSION &

PURSUE YOUR SIDE HUSTLE

(KINDLE, PAPERBACK, AUDIOBOOK)

THE PRODUCTIVE BITE-SIZED ENTREPRENEUR:

24 SMART SECRETS TO DO MORE IN LESS TIME

(KINDLE, PAPERBACK, AUDIOBOOK)

THE BALANCED BITE-SIZED ENTREPRENEUR:

18 BUSINESS STRATEGIES TO HARMONIZE YOUR

LIFE, LOVE & PURPOSE

(KINDLE, PAPERBACK, AUDIOBOOK)

SELECTED BOOKS BY THE AUTHOR

THE ULTIMATE BITE-SIZED ENTREPRENEUR TRILOGY

OUR VIRTUAL SHADOW:

WHY WE ARE OBSESSED WITH DOCUMENTING OUR LIVES ONLINE

PORN & PONG:

HOW GRAND THEFT AUTO, TOMB RAIDER AND OTHER SEXY GAMES CHANGED OUR CULTURE

PLAYBOY'S GREATEST COVERS

Why This Book Shouldn't Exist

This book almost didn't happen. The first THE BITE-SIZED ENTREPRENEUR book came quickly, as did THE PRODUCTIVE BITE-SIZED ENTREPRENEUR. I had just sold my startup, Cuddlr, after an 11-month run as co-founder, and spent a year writing about my experiences for Inc. Magazine, specifically leading a high-profile startup while being a fully-present, hands-on stay-at-home dad of a baby. There was a lot to say! Fresh from Silicon Valley, the belief was that you could not succeed as an entrepreneur and maintain a romantic partnership, nevertheless a family. I wanted to show people that it was possible.

And then, suddenly, I was done.

The first book rocketed up to the top of the Amazon Entrepreneurship books, with the second one following behind, and I began juggling media interviews and requests along with the writing, the consulting and the entrepreneurial advising – you know, how I actually made a living. And I'm still a stay-at-home dad with a new toddler and, now, another son.

I had to make a choice: Focus on the goal of completing the trilogy or admit that the goal didn't fit my new world. So, I'm going to kill myself to write THE BALANCED BITE-SIZED ENTREPRENEUR?

"How absurd", I told my closest confidantes, "for me to burn myself out writing a book about creating balance."

So, I stopped.

In retrospect, it wasn't a stop, but rather a thoughtful pause. Much has happened in the year since the last BITE-SIZED ENTREPRENEUR, but most of it was internal. I learned how to be fully present for two kids, pay more attention to my body (the first books talked about me waking up at 3:15 am to lead my company – and the aftermath), and become grateful for the bit of wisdom I was able to share already in the best-selling books.

More importantly, I began listening to you. I lean towards strategy, so I had all the books planned out, from general launch dates to major discussion points. What I didn't realize until my pause is that you, not me, would tell me what you need. You tell me how I can best serve you.

I traveled the world speaking about THE BITE-SIZED ENTREPRENEUR methods, from Durham, NC, to Bogota, Colombia, to my previous hometown of San Diego. What's amazing was that I'd get the same two questions:

"Do I have enough (time, money, resources, etc.) to start?" and "How do I balance everything in my life with this new thing?"

I always respond to the first question quickly, drawing in the topics of starting small, ideally as a side hustle, and organizing your life based on priorities, to maximize productivity. It's the first two books! Maintaining, though, was what you really needed. Sure, you can get started and have your prioritizes in order. *But if you don't have some sense of balance, then all the resources, time, or passion in the world won't bring you closer to your success.*

Therefore, THE BALANCED BITE-SIZED ENTREPRENEUR goes deeper. How do you manage within chaos? How do you know what to focus on? How do you know when to quit? There are no easy answers, nor should there be. If you haven't already, read through the first two books, particularly the original THE BITE-SIZED ENTREPRENEUR, to build a strong foundation for the concepts addressed here. You should know why persistence always trumps patience and why "No" is the absolute best word for your growth.

And, after reading this book, you'll have a better sense of how to maintain that beautiful structure and mindset you established based on the first two in the trilogy. This third book wouldn't have been possible without me spending a year growing enough to write it. I hope it was worth the wait for you. It was for me.

-Damon Brown, October 2017

I: L̲ET̲ G̲O̲

"All spiritual traditions emphasize the need to keep your attention in the present time. As long as you remain present, everything you need is present with you."

-Caroline Myss, Sacred Contracts

1
THE 3-MINUTE RULE
A few focused minutes will change your entire day

Our attention spans are arguably getting shorter, but our need for depth is growing larger. It does not feel like enough to commit a little or to make small edits. Today, we have romanticized the broad stroke, the sweeping changes, and the dramatic declaration. Perhaps it isn't that our attention spans are lesser, but rather that a remarkable amount of things are clamoring for our attention, and that, to paraphrase both futurist Jared Lanier and iconic entrepreneur Seth Godin, is too much for our lizard brains to handle.

In other words, we feel like we have to make dramatic shifts to make any type of long-lasting impact on our lives.

The good news is that we can push slowly and confidently to our goals. We can take little steps, so small that they're almost unperceivable in our daily lives, but they will significantly change our insight, our strength, and our overall viewpoint.

Here's what you can do in three minutes a day.

Meditation
I started when I moved to New Orleans. I felt like I need to get quiet, not on the outside (NoLa is never a quiet place!), but on the inside. So I sat in my little bed, crossed my legs, and just closed my eyes. I repeated the same thing nearly every day since 2004.

The catch is that my practice is three minutes. I'll occasionally do five minutes on rough days, when I feel like I can't sit still, or on great days, when I actually crave the silence. Just recently, I tried doing twice a day: Midmorning, after I get our youngest son down for his first nap, and mid-evening, after I get our youngest down for his sleep.

The key is that it is so tiny that it has stayed with me, from being a young man escaping Hurricane Katrina to working as a full-time journalist living in downtown San Francisco to becoming a new entrepreneur (and dad) in San Diego to, now, living and working as a veteran stay-at-home dad and consultant in Toledo, Ohio. I can *always* spare three minutes to sit. You can, too.

Goal setting
Poker champion Phil Hellmuth wrote his six major life goals on a piece of paper and put it on his bathroom mirror. He hit five out of six within a few years, including winning the World Series of Poker. Entrepreneur Elon Musk put his goal for the electric car on a random Tumblr blog and, ten years later, Tesla was the leader in that vehicle space.

I write down my goals on index cards,

sometimes once a quarter, sometimes once a year, often with a deadline. It takes three minutes to jot them down. In 2014, I did a TED talk about the power of index cards, which was nine minutes longer than the time I take to write down my ideas. Chances are you already know what you want. Write it down. It won't take long.

A few things happen when you put it down on paper. First, you are forced to articulate your vision, which makes it more concrete than something floating in your mind. Second, you've got a compass to guide all your decisions. Got a new opportunity? If it doesn't fit into your ultimate goals, then it can (and should) be a quick "No". Third, as the late motivational speaker Jim Rohn said, you can actually keep track of your growth. What were your goals a year ago? If you don't know, then you can't see – or celebrate – how much you've grown.

Again, three minutes of your time.

Enjoy your environment
Consider the world your playground. For me, it hit me when we had our first kid, and those daily miles-long walks I took to clear my mind had become unrealistic. Instead, my exercise and motion had to come from pacing carrying my son, walking while I was on the phone, or, later, pushing his stroller up and down San Diego hills.

What I began to do is savor such opportunities to move more. I'd travel through airports and take the stairs rather than the escalator. Later, when I'd have the time during layovers, I'd skip the people mover and even the trains to briskly walk to the next terminal. These bite-sized improvements led to me getting in some of the best shape of my life, despite the natural chaos of running an ambitious home career with two young kids.

For you, it could be parking a little further from the grocery store, skipping the elevator in two story buildings, or other small changes. When you move, your body doesn't only appreciate it, but your mind relishes it, too. Great strategies and new ideas have come to me while I was walking, including this very book series.

Consistent action, not dramatic action, fuels growth.

2
YOU NEED LONGER DEADLINES
Unnecessary pressure often creates disappointing results

It is Monday morning and I already experienced a failure this week. I have a product I worked hard to finish and roll out today, but the pieces didn't come together on time. It was sometime mid-Sunday, shortly after lunch that I realized I'd have to suck it up and let it go.

What is fascinating is that there was no reason for my new product to launch today. No one, aside from a couple confidants, knew it was going to launch. In fact, my work would probably go on fine without it. Coincidentally, just a few weeks ago, someone in my brain trust suggested I try to let go of "false deadlines".

A false deadline is a hard stop you give yourself for some inconsequential reason. It could be to placate your ego, it could be you want to get a project off your plate, it could be you're just sick of looking at it on your ever-growing to-do list. The fact is that it actually doesn't matter: You have no external pressure to perform. It is all internal.

Can you relate? Here's how I calm myself down when I see myself setting up (and failing) a false deadline.

Where did this deadline come from?
If you pause for a second, then you may find the origin of your deadline isn't even relevant anymore. I've worked on projects where the aggressive timeline was based on another department's needs - yet when the other group pushed its timeline out, we didn't change ours! The result was we were rushing around for quite literally nothing.

When did this deadline become a priority?
I'm a big advocate for not waiting until tomorrow to create the life you want, but it is just as important to know today what moves are *ideal* and what moves are *necessary*. An ideal goal can sneak into the necessary goal category and, suddenly, the amount of pressure you give yourself to reach this ambitious end is significantly higher. I help others increase their productivity and I still struggle with this phenomenon.

What will happen if you don't meet this goal?
This last point is critical, as you have to be able to identify what you fear will happen if you don't meet this false deadline. You can't process the anxiety around meeting the deadline if you don't know what, exactly, you are feeling.

For me, I'm proud of what I've created, so missing today's deadline means I have to wait longer to share it. Disappointing? Definitely. Career threatening? Far from it. And oftentimes, when I have missed a false deadline, opportunities to make the product greater pop up after the fact - making the temporary pain all the more worthwhile. It's just a matter of remember this *while* it is happening.

3
PUT YOUR MASK ON FIRST
Assume tomorrow won't provide your rest

There's a reason we are comfortable sacrificing it all to make our businesses a reality: We assume we'll get a break tomorrow. To paraphrase Orphan Annie, tomorrow is always a day away--but meanwhile we could end up being useless to the very people we say we are sacrificing everything for.

Consultant Alan Weiss calls this the Oxygen Mask Principle. If you're in an emergency situation on an airplane, you are told to put your oxygen mask on first before assisting a less competent companion. He breaks it down in his podcast, *The Way I See It*:

You can't help the client or your family, you can't do pro bono work, you can't help others in the profession, you can't help anyone unless you yourself are comfortable. You need a healthy selfishness.

Weiss wrote *Value-Based Fees,* one of my favorite business books, and it is refreshing to hear such a driven businessman discuss the need for balance. As I talked about in THE PRODUCTIVE BITE-SIZED ENTREPRENEUR, being busy does not equal productivity--and continuous exhaustion will not only make your work sloppy but ultimately wreck both you and your business.

Ironically, prioritizing your self-care is the best way to take care of others. How are you taking care of yourself today?

4
CHECK THE WEATHER
Even the best effort is a waste when the timing is wrong

Life is probably significantly different for you now than it was five years ago, one year ago, or maybe even one month ago. This sentiment remains strong for me, especially in the wake of a cross-country move, but other reasons have been encouraging me to think about change lately. Returning to the Midwest, where I had lived during my teenage years, means trading a decade of neutral West Coast seasons for the gorgeous, crisp turning of the leaves. Winter actually feels intimidating now, but not because I'm afraid of the cold (my biggest TED Talk was in wintery Whistler, British Columbia, Canada). Rather, the prospect of shorter days and frigid nights makes me feel closer to nature, as if, post-California, I am suddenly exposed after being sheltered away from the rest of the world.

It feels invigorating to follow the flow of the seasons and actually, consciously, let things naturally whither away. Ideas that later became principles and passions that became dogma. The pursuit of a big, hairy, ambitious goal became the focus rather than the original reason why I created the goal in the first place. For many reasons, big goals that I set for myself as recently as a year ago now seem almost silly. Contrary to common belief, it is not easier to give up. It is actually easier to keep fighting because at least you feel like you're making progress.

When you pause, though, you can see how ridiculous it feels planting a tomato seed during an ice storm or crossing a raging river when it isn't anywhere near frozen. It's just that, before that quiet moment, you aren't paying attention to the natural flow of your world. You're just trying to reach your goal.

The near-misses, almost-wases, and should-have-beens have been plentiful lately and, frankly, feel more robust than they've been in my life in a long while. So do the coincidences and absolutes, as if fate stepped in and said 'Nah, you're going that way. I'll make sure of that!' It pleases my ego to say that I am one determined individual, which is why life has to react so forcefully when I should be going in a different direction. And, as the world slows down and I slowly get over myself, I am becoming amazed at how, to paraphrase Steve Jobs, seemingly random dots of events begin to form a pattern.

But you can only see the evidence when you're looking back. Going forward requires trusting that fall will follow summer. And it always does.

5
FAILURE CAN BE SUCCESS
Holding your nose during a failure misses the point

Failure is a prerequisite for getting what you want, and often it puts us in the direction to get what we actually need. It gave Apple's Steve Jobs a mission, Shark Tank's Daymond John a vision, and every entrepreneur you know a groundedness not achievable otherwise. To paraphrase Brené Brown, the only guarantee you have when you step in the arena is that you will get your butt kicked.

So when one of the most successful women in the world talks about her failures, it is wise to listen.

In 1998, Oprah Winfrey's big-budget movie *Beloved* was set to be her splash into Hollywood. Her agent called her the day after opening night and told her it was already a flop. She was devastated.

Two decades later, she is even more powerful than before. How does that happen? There are three telling quotes:

Gratitude
"That's when the gratitude practice became really strong for me, because it's hard to remain sad if you're focused on what you have instead of what you don't have."

There are volumes of anecdotal and scientific evidence showing that gratitude for what you currently have leads to your getting more of what you want. Your brain focuses on what you focus on, so concentrating on what's missing will only show you what you lack, not the new opportunities available.

Service
"It taught me to never again--never again, ever--put all of your hopes, expectations, eggs in the basket of box office. Do the work as an offering, and then whatever happens, happens."

Your job is to create something that the world needs -- and that's it. Profitability comes from prioritizing your employees and your customers, not from prioritizing profitability. Market share comes from creating a service of value, not from focusing on market share. In Oprah's case, she gives and gives, and her customers choose to give their financial, emotional, and mental support in return.

Presence
"There's not a human being alive who doesn't want--in any conversation, encounter, experience with another human being--to feel like they matter. And you can resolve any issue if you could just get to what it is that they want--they want to be

heard. And they want to know that what they said to you meant something. Most people go their entire lives and nobody ever really wants the answer to 'How are you? Tell me about yourself.'"

It is ridiculously easy to depersonalize people because of your goals: networking with someone just to get something out of it, manipulating customers to reach a new milestone, or simply not taking the time to take care of the people who gave you success in the first place.

Gratitude, service, and presence can bring you to your goals -- and help you overcome the many failures it will take to get there.

6
DO GOOD ENOUGH
Perfection prevents greatness

We have a cultural obsession with extreme experiences: Things have to be uber or incredible or outstanding or breathtaking. The obsession pours into our expectations of ourselves, as it isn't enough to get funding, but to be a unicorn, and being a simple company is inadequate compared to being a grand disrupter.

It also means we tend to kill our ideas, if not our own success, before they have a chance to be great.

In praise of good enough

The best thing you can do is go for good. It doesn't mean settling for good when great is available. It means understanding that good is actually good, and that everything you do is intended as a start, not as a permanent state.

Ironically, while Silicon Valley is focused on "crushing it", the popular Lean Startup model is based on the very idea of good enough. In short, you take your idea, create it with as little resources as possible and get your good enough take - your minimal viable product - to your intended audience as quickly as possible.

The problem with high expectations
The feedback from your audience takes your idea from good to great. High expectations alone won't get you there. In fact, high expectations are likely to hamper your progress.

Ryan Holiday and Stephen Hanselman's *The Daily Stoic* explains that most of our frustration isn't with our progress, but with our expectations. We could have extraordinary success yet, if we are expecting an unrealistic amount of progress, that rare success won't even feel like an accomplishment.

The success trap

An excellent cautionary tale is iconic performer Michael Jackson handling the success of his breakthrough album *Thriller*. The late icon worked with megaproducer Quincy Jones and essentially redefined R & B - *Thriller* is still one of the top 20 selling albums of all time. The problem? Jackson wanted to do it again. According to Jones, he spent the rest of his life, album after album, trying to create something bigger than Thriller. As a result, he never felt quite satisfied.

Keep in mind, Jones wasn't saying something equal to *Thriller*. Something more successful than *Thriller*. One of the best-selling albums of all time.

The Atlantic explained the challenge during the 25th anniversary of *Bad*, the critically-panned *Thriller* follow-up:

Jackson in interviews more often expressed Olympian commercial goals of breaking the sales records of his previous album than he did of pursuing new musical territory. And very much like how many filmmakers of blockbusters beef up defining fight scenes and plotlines, Jackson conspicuously restaged and amplified Thriller's signature moments with perfectionist's precision, making Bad sound sterile in too many places.

It is an amazing trap: You naturally hit a home run and, next time up to bat, you're checking wind conditions, wearing a lucky hat and trying to recreate the previous experience.

The rub is that what you did - the success you had - wasn't just based on your actions. It is both timing and inspiration, too. The sales success of *Thriller* could not be recreated because the whole record industry sold less records, as we would see with Napster and iTunes and Spotify. The needs of the listeners changed (ironically, because of *Thriller* itself), so doing another *Thriller* wouldn't recreate the same sea change. And Jackson was arguably in a different place, as he now had ridiculously high expectations of himself and a new set of pressures.

Lightning won't strike in the same place twice

Sometimes we expect to do the same amazing work twice, so we get sloppy the second time around. Just as often, though, we can give ourselves too much credit for our success, overanalyzing what we did initially as if our win was completely based on our actions.

It is wiser to be humble and focused rather than just expecting an unlikely win. And in a true Zen way, setting smaller, realistic goals leads us bigger long-term success.

When Oprah Winfrey asked author Paulo Coehlo if he was intimidated by the phenomenal success of *The Alchemist*, he replied, "*The Alchemist* was a one-time thing." The Alchemist, selling 65 million copies worldwide, was only Coehlo's second book. He just published his 31st one.

You can be paralyzed or you can be grateful.

7
KNOW YOUR SACRIFICE
Know when you're going to quit ahead of time

Quitting is severely underrated. If you've been following entrepreneurial leadership, then you know that everyone from Steve Jobs to the Google founders built their success on quitting. So why are we obsessed with making things work instead of just accepting that some of our ideas have run their course?

On its decade anniversary, it is worth taking another read of business maverick Seth Godin's classic *The Dip: A Little Book That Teaches You When to Quit (And When to Stick)*. I just rediscovered *The Dip* on audiobook, and perhaps the biggest insight we can all use is this:

Write down under what circumstances you're willing to quit.

To explain, Godin quotes ultramarathoner Dick Collins: "Decide before the race the conditions that will cause you to decide to stop and drop out. You don't want to be out there saying, 'Well, gee, my leg hurts, I'm a little dehydrated, I'm sleepy, I'm tired, and it's cold, and it's windy...' and talk yourself into quitting."

If you're making a decision based on how you're feeling at that moment, then you will probably make the wrong decision.

You don't quit when the going gets rough. You quit when you know you've invested more than you'll get out of it. You need clear, measurable metrics to know when to give up on your big idea or business.

Here are a few I've recently used:

I'll spend this much money

I self-financed THE BITE-SIZED ENTREPRENEUR: 21 WAYS TO IGNITE YOUR PASSION AND PURSUE YOUR SIDE HUSTLE. I set a budget and a timeline to recoup that money. It hit the Amazon Entrepreneur book Top 10, which helped me reach the goal and do a follow-up book, THE PRODUCTIVE BITE-SIZED ENTREPRENEUR: 24 SMART SECRETS TO DO MORE IN LESS TIME. If I didn't recoup, then there would be no follow up – and you wouldn't be reading this book right now!

I'll spend this much time

I spent a good amount of time on a side hustle and gave myself a few months to make it work. And, with no fanfare, I recently shut it down. Why? Come to find out, no one wanted it. To paraphrase Godin, the temporary pain of giving up is better than the slow death of mindlessly continuing.

I'll spend this much effort

I love working on new ideas, and there is one that I had been toiling away on for years. Within the last few days, I realized that the effort is too great to make it real based on my current time, priorities and resources. It sucks, but moving forward with it begs the question: How much of my life would I have to put in upheaval to make this thing a reality and, if I see myself at the finish line, would it have been worth it?

Give yourself permission to say, "No, it isn't worth it." And give yourself permission *before* you actually start.

8
THE ULTIMATE TIME LIMIT
Always remember your time can end at any moment

There is a simple reason why we procrastinate: We assume we will have more time. There is more time to make it perfect, more time to connect with others and more time to pursue that brilliant idea. But success lies in knowing that time will run out - and that we will die.

In two decades, successful entrepreneur Ricardo Semler turned Semco Partners from a four million-dollar company to a $212 million company - namely by creating an intuitive, innovative work environment, shared in his best-selling book *Maverick*. Semler is also a very happy man, but he says it has nothing to do with his financial or business success. As he recently explained to Tim Ferriss, Semler's real secret is treating each day as his last.

I kept thinking 'Geez, I don't want to be in that situation where suddenly now I have to go to ballgames with the kids and I have to travel to places I haven't been and I have to write that play that I never wrote.' That's crazy. Let's do something else... So, on Mondays and Thursdays I have what I call 'Terminal Days', the two days a week in which my schedule is completely clear and I do on those days what I would have done if I heard this conversation from my oncologist.

This habit isn't just for show. Semler says melanoma runs in his family, so most of his relatives have a sudden death. He himself has had multiple cancer surgeries that, fortunately, caught the melanoma before it spread. Even though he is 57, Semler faces his own death every day.

Semler sets aside two days a week to do exactly what he would do if it were the last day of his life. It is easy to assume that his work would suffer, but, in fact, he is regularly setting himself up for career greatness. Think about it: If you actually carved out time for personal fulfillment every single week, imagine how focused and productive you would be during the remaining days?

For the ambitious among us, our problem isn't saying "Yes" (as Shonda Rhimes said in her TED Talk), but in saying "No". You have to close a number of doors to truly do what you desire - and material or worldly success only increases the choices over time, making the process even more difficult.

Start making tough decisions now before they get tougher over time. What should you be focusing on today?

9
THE BIGGEST CHANGES
Like icebergs, most of our growth happens below the surface

It has been a summer of transitions for most people I know, myself included. My family and I recently moved to the Midwest after spending a dozen years on the West Coast. I'm fortunate that my focus, on helping potential and current entrepreneurs reach their best without burning themselves out, only gets richer as I connect with new communities in the Toledo/Detroit area.

Any transition takes a great deal of energy, no matter how advantageous or exciting it may be. It is like what writer Elizabeth Gilbert said in one of my favorite talks I've ever seen at TED: Her stratospheric success with *Eat, Pray, Love* caused the same performance anxiety as when she was a waitressing wannabe writer collecting hundreds of publishing rejection letters. Both felt like a foreign place. Her way back to sanity? She started writing the next thing. She did the work.

The key during transitions isn't just to keep your focus, but to realize that it will take you more energy to do so. Like moving to a new town, previously unconscious acts like going to the grocery store or remembering a neighbor's name now require thought, rigor, and presence. You are building the foundation for your next chapter. Most importantly, you are given the opportunity to think about the things you previously assumed to be true and can make a structure better for you today.

All this takes time, all this takes energy, and all this takes patience. So, I'm allowing myself a few extra minutes of meditation each day, an additional breath or two before returning an urgent phone call, and considerable thoughtfulness in my workday strategy. The best gift you can give yourself is the space to get the inner work done to make a stronger you - even if you are the only one who can feel it. You are doing more work than you think.

II: Take In

"For every single thing you want in life, there's a price; a price that has to be paid. And nature always demands that the price be paid in advance."

— Brian Tracy, *How to Start and Succeed in Your Own Business*

10
EVERY SINGLE DAY
Habits become your life

It's been proven that rituals and habits are the key to success. I meditate nearly every morning. I listen to something thoughtful daily, most recently *The Daily Stoic*. I always walk as much as possible. Still, the rapid evolution of my career gives me days where I question the very point of having these routines. I'm still struggling.

If you can relate, then it is key to remind yourself that practices are the foundation for those very times when you feel like things are going out of control. They are the structures upon which your stability sits.

I often think of an old *SPIN* magazine article featuring River Cuomo, the self-described temperamental leader of the alternative band Weezer. The feature talked about Cuomo taking up meditation, going deep into self-discovery and so on. When asked about how he changed, a band member captured the general sentiment well. To paraphrase:

He's still a [explicative]. But imagine how much of a bigger [explicative] he'd be without doing this?

It's not that waking up early, always making your bed or writing down your gratitude will make you transcend disappointment, heartache and failure. It's that your routines will make you more *resilient* to face those obstacles. And, over time, they have a cumulative effect on your life, like compound interest in the bank.

Pause before you consider subtracting habits out of your life because the results seem invisible. Instead, they could be keeping you afloat and keeping you from going further off your course.

11
CARRY ONE THING AT A TIME
Guilt over focusing on one thing will make you useless at all things

I remember the moment I realized it wasn't going to work. I was in New York, visiting to support a local TED conference, and it hit me that I would not be able to fulfill my new desire: Becoming a worldwide public speaker. My newborn son was at home, along with my toddler, and we crammed together a patchwork of support to cover my absence as the primary caregiver. It required a redeye to even get my day in Manhattan. I'd be flying home that same night, hopefully getting some shuteye at the airport while I waited to board. My boys needed me. My heart needed to be on the road.

Before I left, I had a tea with my friend and mentor, artist Leida Snow. I talked about my ambitions, my opportunities, and my conflict. She smiled, and talked for a bit. This is what I understood:

Balance isn't doing everything at once. Balance is doing what is most important at the time. Sometimes you'll be super present as a dad. Sometimes you'll be super present as an international speaker. It's OK to put one down and pick the other one up. But you can't be both at the same moment.

It reminds me of Buddhist monk Thich Nhat Hanh, whom often talks about anticipation and anxiety for the future (which is the same thing) robbing the pleasure out of an experience when it actually does happen. Or my own research for my book Our Virtual Shadow: Why We Are Obsessed with Documenting Our Lives Online, where we pull ourselves out of the moment to capture the moment and, in a sense, don't experience the moment at all.

Bifurcating myself would make me a bad father and a bad public speaker, as I wouldn't be fully invested in either.

Instead, when I was at home, my family would have my love and attention, and when I hit the stage, my audience would have me totally engaged in the conversation. It honors me, it honors you, and it honors my family.

Or, as Hanh puts it, "Do one thing at a time. Do it deeply."

12

BUILD LIKE YOU'RE ALREADY THERE

Focus on the small and the big will handle itself

The late, powerful speaker Jim Rohn helped guide Tony Robbins' early career and, as you can imagine, was a force unto himself. A quote from one of Rohn's classic talks is still relevant, if not more so today:

"You say, 'If I had a big organization, you know, I'd really run it with a strong hand and I'd be a fabulous leader. But I've only got a few (followers) and I don't know where they are.' See, that's not going to work. If you wish to preside over a lot... you have to be disciplined when the amounts are small."

What Rohn is talking about is *systems*: A system to master your emotional intelligence so you can handle the power; a system to handle your relationships so your management can scale; and a system to organize your resources so you can use them most effectively in high numbers.

The thing is that those systems can most easily be put into place when the overhead is as low as the stakes. Ironically, as Rohn mentions, it's easy to not take the systems seriously when the rewards are weak, yet this is the very time you should be thinking about long-range goals.

It's kind of like wishing to win the lottery, but not actually thinking about what you would do with the money: The chances of you wasting the money if you got it are extremely high. And even if you did have a plan, if you didn't manage things well on the small scale, you certainly wouldn't have the discipline to do it with millions!

Entrepreneurs often learn this the hard way. How many companies end up growing faster than expected, becoming worth billions in a few short years, only to do expensive fixes because they didn't take the time to consider details that felt virtually inconsequential when they were small?

Instead, take a step today - even a small one - to put a system in place so you will be able to better emotionally, relationally and financially handle your business if and when it does reach new heights. It is often more dangerous to prepare for failure than it is for success.

13
THE 20/20 TECHNIQUE
Make the most of your time and of others

The further you get in your field, the more thoughtful you have to be about the time you spend. It often means saying "No" more than you would like. Former Googler Jenny Blake, author of the best-selling book *Pivot*, has a great way to defend your time and help other people.

When someone asks for a brain picking session, Blake instead suggests they do a 20/20 meeting (I interpreted it as 20/20, but the numbers can be higher or lower). The meeting is 20 minutes talking about what you care about and then 20 minutes talking about what the other person cares about.

I love this method for many reasons:

Eliminate the one-way conversation
Blake has a best-selling book, a significant career at the most envied startup in the world and a reputation for helping people get their businesses to the next level. You have your own expertise, too, and it would be too easy for you to give and not receive, especially as you gain prominence in your field. By splitting the time evenly, you remove potential one-sidedness.

Prevent takers from monopolizing time
There are many reasons why people may feel comfortable monopolizing your time, from feeling like you owe them to listen to being just thoughtless about your other obligations. By declaring a split meeting, you create equal expectations from the outset and make it clear that you expect to be receiving value from the meeting, too. Their reaction to your suggestion makes their intentions clearer and can help you decide whether you want to actually spend more time with the person.

Smooth out the power dynamics

Everyone you meet has a piece of insight that can help you or has access to people or social circles that can be beneficial to your business. How do you know if you're the only one giving insight? Instead, the 20/20 rule gives you and your companion equal footing, potentially staving off weird power dynamics and giving both of you an opportunity for growth. And after the meeting, they don't owe you anything, just as you don't owe them anything either.

14
THEORY IS JUST THAT
Don't mistake an idea for a solution

You'd be forgiven for not immediately associating former heavyweight boxing champion Mike Tyson with emotional intelligence, especially if, like me, you remember his more ferocious years. However, he's always had a strong sensitivity and insight under the tough veneer, as shown in documentaries like *Tyson*.

He also has one of the wisest quotes you'll ever hear on how to make emotionally intelligent decisions as an entrepreneur, if not as a human being.

"Everybody has a plan until they get punched in the mouth."

Accurate. His famous quote obviously leans on the ring analogy, but it applies well to your business strategy. Here is the two-part blow-by-blow.

Assume you will fail

Tyson is talking about the hubris behind our strategies. We've got millions of dollars in investment from the top VCs? That doesn't mean you go on cruise control. (If anything, as Mark Cuban says, you've just made the road to success longer) We raised a ton on Kickstarter? That's just the first step of many - and one misstep could knock us off balance.

The best defense is to assume you will get hit: Critics will drag you, ideas will fail to launch and burnout is real. Your strategy isn't a bulletproof dome protecting you from crisis, but rather a foundation that allows you to keep it together during the inevitable challenges.

Plan to the end

Tyson is explaining that you need to have a strategy deeper than the one in your head, as you are going to get frustrated as soon as you hit a stumbling block. Have you ever prepared for a confrontation by guessing what's going to happen? We're usually way off, as we are skimming over many different chaotic factors like the environment and our opponent's state of mind. Worse, by planning too much ahead of time, we are closing ourselves off to potentially better plans we develop based on insights we only see once we get in the proverbial ring.

The best plan is to focus on outcome. How do you want this thing to end? By focusing on the finish line and the important milestones along the way, you give yourself the latitude to get there based on the most practical moves of that dynamic moment. Think about boxing, where a quick hit could swell your eye shut, weaken your arm or literally take your breath away. The ability to pivot quickly without going over the emotional deep end is vital to your success.

There is a reason why every classic strategy book from *The Art of War* to *The 48 Laws of Power* emphasize planning to the end as well as assuming you will not always win. As Tyson knows, the ultimate personal emotional intelligence happens when you accept you don't know what's going to happen next.

15
DOING THEIR BEST
When we undervalue others, we inevitable undervalue ourselves, too

Every entrepreneur learns quickly that creating your own path doesn't make you less reliant on others. In fact, it is the reverse: While a traditional corporate job may hand you one boss, entrepreneurship requires building and maintaining a healthy relationship with co-founders, customers, funders, mentors, and many others.

And the truth is that you won't always like the people you need. Emotional intelligence guru Brené Brown has a quick way to help you get even the most challenging relationship back on track:

The most compassionate people ... assume that other people are doing the best they can. I lived the opposite way: I assumed that people weren't doing their best, so I judged them and constantly fought being disappointed ...

The next time you get frustrated with someone, ask a simple question: Do you believe the person is doing the very best that he or she can?

What often happens is that we realize how much we are judging someone on the basis of our own skills, experience, and strengths. For instance, I have spent decades doing non-traditional work, so I have the discipline to stay focused in unusual work environments such as my home office or in an airplane while traveling. Some people fall apart under the same circumstances, either because they are new to the situation or just have a different personality. Are they doing the best they can, even if the results are poor? In most cases, yes, they are.

Try applying this simple question to the co-worker who always seems to fumble, the family member who regularly disappoints you, or the customer who seems rather dense. As Brown points out in her book *Rising Strong*, the result is empathy--empathy for the fact that they, too, are doing the best they can with what they've got. It opens up possibilities that you would be closed off to otherwise.

And while becoming a more empathic person is a smart relationship builder, the biggest impact may end up being on you: If you are more accepting of others, then you inevitably become more gentle with yourself.

16
IT ISN'T YOUR MONEY
More resources will just make you more of what you already are now

Podcasts to me, like for millions of people, have become an amazing staple this year. Forget TV: Podcasts are my episodic content. Tara Gentile's *Profit Power Pursuit*, Reid Hoffman's *Masters of Scale*, and NPR's *How I Built This* have transformed my business.

One of the most valuable podcast episodes you can listen to, though, is Basecamp and Ruby on Rails founder David Heinemeier Hansson on *The Tim Ferriss Show*. It is a monster of a conversation, clocking in at three and a half hours and touching on everything from smart productivity to brilliant learning strategies to startup mistakes.

The absolute best reason to listen is this gem:

Expectations, not outcomes, govern the happiness of your perceived reality

The line is originally from Heinemeier's own stellar piece about becoming a millionaire in *The Observer*. He and Ferriss spend a significant amount of time breaking down exactly what it means.

Here are three high-level lessons, though you'll want to listen to the whole discussion:

Develop skillsets necessary for after you "make it"

If you are doing 100-hour weeks, sacrificing time with friends and family and not developing any other interests aside from your business, then how do you expect to be happy once you sell your business and suddenly have a life composed of only undeveloped friends and family relationships and withered interests?

Maintain your outside pursuits, however minor the effort. In my own case, selling my first startup didn't land me in early retirement, but it did bring up many emotional issues on how a major part of my life was now gone. Imagine if it had been longer than a year of my life - and imagine if I had sacrificed being a present father, husband and friend along the way.

Your sacrifice now doesn't increase your chances of happiness later
Heinemeier notes that he and Basecamp co-founder Jason Fried manage the wildly successful company on a 40-hour a week schedule. Forty hours! There are administrative assistants who clock in more hours. Heinemeier, Ferriss and even I have met many an entrepreneur who believe sacrificing everything for seven to 10 years means you'll find success and the ever-elusive happiness at the end. But there is no guarantee that you'll live to see it, nor that it will actually be there when you get there.

Now is all you've got. If your quality of life sucks now, then, after a decade, you'll be in the habit of burnout, hypertension, depression, or any number of aliments your body has become accustomed to. Better to take things day by day and pull in as much enjoyment within the time you have, which is a major premise of Heinemeier and Fried's wonderful title *Rework* as well as this very book.

Focus on process, not success
Success is often a deceptively vague outcome. If your goal is to be rich, then do you have a number in mind, and rich compared to whom, exactly? If your goal is to be famous, then is it to the world, to strangers on the street or to a handful of people who matter to you? And, as I've confessed recently, reaching goals is elusive because ambitious people always move the goal post as soon as they near reaching it.

Focus on the parts of the journey/struggle that motivate you, as they will be the same whether you have financial success or not. Heinemeier says that he enjoys himself the most when nurturing his now-ubiquitous programming language Ruby on Rails or working with his long-time business partner Fried - just like, as he notes, when he was broke living in a tiny Copenhagen apartment. The happiest among us do what we love now because we recognize where we feel the most alive, and, for better or worse, recognize that money won't change that basic principle.

17

YOU ARE ALREADY SUCCESSFUL
You're making more progress than you think

Many of us sit in one of two types of reality-distortion fields. You may think you are more successful than you really are, which means you're in danger of not accomplishing much. Or you may think you aren't doing enough, which means you may burn yourself out because you think you have further to go. If you are an ambitious businessperson, then by definition you are the latter. It fuels you. It also can destroy you.

Long-time author Jeanette Hurt and I have talked about this for years: We are driven to an incredibly high goal, and just as it is clear we will reach it, we move the flagpole further down the line. Unfortunately, that means never quite being satisfied, nor actually giving oneself credit.

Your insatiable appetite for goal setting may drive you forward, but there's no danger in tempering that trait with some checks and balances. Here's what you can do.

Celebrate every victory
When I launched THE BITE-SIZED ENTREPRENEUR and THE PRODUCTIVE BITE-SIZED ENTREPRENEUR, I actually wrote down simple rewards I would give myself at certain sales numbers. I initially had super high markers, but I forced myself to make the victories low. It forced me into the routine of celebrating even minor wins - making the book process even more joyful this time around.

Lean on others
It is essential that you have a small group of people who know your intent and are invested in having you reach your goals. I call them a brain trust, as I've talked about before (Jeanette Hurt is

part of mine). When you're not recognizing the success you've made, your brain trust will bring you down to earth and remind you that you did reach your goal - you just decided to move the flag.

Make realistic goals

The further the space between you and your goal, the longer it will feel like you aren't achieving much. Realistic milemarkers not only give you a system to recognize your success, but they also increase the chances of you reaching those momentous goals - since you will have the motivation to complete them from all the minor successes along the way.

18
MIND THE GAP
The space between giant leaps makes the giant leaps happen

Silence often breeds discontent, then enlightenment. I've found that the best thoughts aren't in the hectic speed of the day, the pushing towards bigger ideas or the relentless drive towards superior results. No, the challenge isn't doing the grind for another day – at least for me. The real discipline comes with navigating the space in between, the netherland between doing and not doing, the uncomfortable area that shows no results nor failure.

That uncomfortable space could be when you stop talking about your idea, between the newlywed excitement of a new idea and the actual prototype that you have to share. It can be the time between you launching a rough sketch and you refining the next version, since you have nothing new to show. It could be after your big success and, alas, your next idea is still a sketch on an index card, a document or even just in your brain.

What matters is persevering within that area, that gap, until you make it to the other side. Grinding it out is really easy. So is quitting. But both are smart when done in moderation, but foolish when used as a rule, as either extreme will not get the job done. Instead, it is a matter of breathing in, taking in the vagueness, and accepting that the gap, too, is an equal part of the process.

Sometimes taking a breath isn't a limbo before your next act. Sometimes taking a breath *is* your next act.

Let's Connect!

This book is just the beginning of your growth. Here's how we keep THE BITE-SIZED ENTREPRENEUR conversation going.

Do the Bite-Sized Entrepreneur Boot Camp
http://www.bsbootcamp.com

This six-part, self-guided course will bring the best out of your current productivity, focus, and creativity. Taking the book series a step further, THE BITE-SIZED ENTREPRENEUR boot camp is perfect to do at your own pace with my guidance through video, audio, and text. Join through JoinDamon.me to get a special discount on the course and even some one-on-one coaching opportunities!

Get Bonus Content & More
http://www.JoinDamon.me

Get your free BITE-SIZED ENTREPRENEUR toolkit to gain even more insight into your next steps. You'll also get exclusive content, early previews of new goodies, and more!

ONE-ON-ONE BITE-SIZED GUIDANCE
http://www.damonbrown.net

I'd love to help you organize your priorities, apply THE BITE-SIZED ENTREPRENEUR method, and make room for your best career. We can set up a time to chat and see if we're a good fit. Reach out at damon@damonbrown.net.

SPEAKING AT YOUR EVENT
http://www.damonbrown.net

I am happy to talk about your event and how a discussion on mindfulness, productivity, or entrepreneurship can best fit your needs. International venues are welcome, as are American events, and my platforms include TED, Colombia 4.0 in Bogota, and American University in Washington D.C. My keynote talks are also available and discussed in detail on the next section, **AVAILABLE KEYNOTE TALKS**.

Available Keynote Talks

Damon is available to speak worldwide at select events, conferences, and companies. His audiences have included the main TED Conference, second stage, in British Columbia, American Underground tech incubator in Durham, NC, Colombia 4.0 in Bogota, Colombia, the Adult Entertainment Expo in Las Vegas, and American University in Washington D.C. Damon's talks interweave personal narrative and industry knowledge with actionable strategies. He is also happy to include Q & As and panel discussions.

Watch Damon's speakers reel at http://bit.ly/DamonTalks.
Contact Damon at damon@damonbrown.net.

His three mainstage keynotes are below:

PROFIT
HOW TO CREATE YOUR TRUE WORTH
Creatives often undervalue their services to the market, to their bank account, and to the world. In this inspiration and practical talk, Damon shares the best ways we can joyfully make a living off our craft, create business partnerships worthy of our skills, and truly be of service to others.

ENTREPRENEURSHIP
WHY YOU CAN (AND SHOULD) START YOUR SIDE HUSTLE IMMEDIATELY
Believe it or not, we already have most of the skills we need to create our passion-driven business. So why aren't most people pursuing their potentially profitable ideas? They are intimidated by the small gap in their skill set. In this immediately actionable talk, Damon shares how to easily traverse that gap and explains the three crucial strengths every successful entrepreneur possesses. It is an inspiring talk for both potential entrepreneurs and ambitious upstarts.

Success

Why You Need to Be Global to Succeed Locally

The most exciting business ideas often come from our own needs, but in today's global marketplace, we absolutely must go further than our own backyard to create, test and ultimately deliver to our ultimate customers. Sharing lessons from his own acquired app, Cuddlr, Damon shows the many ways we need to go beyond our social circle (and our comfort zone) to better understand what the market needs and to serve our most important communities.

FIVE MORE GREAT BOOKS TO READ

THE WAR OF ART: BREAK THROUGH THE BLOCKS AND WIN YOUR INNER CREATIVE BATTLES BY STEVEN PRESSFIELD

On the book: What he talks about in the book is something called "Resistance". Resistance is that thing that stops us from spending a little time working on something, the thing that tells us that we're not quite good enough... And the whole book explores how Resistance can be defeated - and how it will never go away.

REWORK BY JASON FRIED & DAVID HEINEMEIER HANSSON

On the book: Before you become successful, use this time to make mistakes without the whole world hearing about them. Keep tweaking. Work out the kinks. Test random ideas. Try new things. No one knows you, so it's no big deal if you mess up.

Pivot: The Only Move That Matters Is Your Next One by Jenny Blake

On the book: Understand that any confusion or trepidation you feel is normal and, as shown in any of the books, there is already a blueprint to your potential success.

Big Magic: Creative Living Beyond Fear by Elizabeth Gilbert

On the book: Being famous or prolific won't help you succeed again. What matters is the work and your intention. Is your product or service being done with the audience at the forefront? Are you contributing something more to the cultural conversation? Ego-driven enterprises rarely rise as high as purely-motivated work - and we are in the most danger of doing the former after a big win.

The Dip: A Little Book That Teaches You When to Quit (and When to Stick) by Seth Godin

On the book: *If you're making a decision based on how you're feeling at that moment, then you will probably make the wrong decision.* You don't quit when the going gets rough. You quit when you know you've invested more than you'll get out of it. You need clear, measurable metrics to know when to give up on your big idea or business.

SIGNIFICANT QUOTES & REFERENCES

- Table of Contents
    - Opening quote: Oprah's Super Soul Conversations podcast, "Phil Jackson: The Soul of Success". Originally aired October 9, 2017.
- I: Let Go:
    - Opening quote: Caroline Myss, *Sacred Contracts: Awakening Your Divine Potential* (Harmony 2002)
- Chapter 2: Put Your Mask on First
    - Adapted from the *Inc.* column "How to Stop Burnout with 1 Simple Rule". Originally published September 28, 2016

- Chapter 3: You Need Longer Deadlines
  - Adapted from the *Inc.* column "How Unnecessarily Ambitious Deadlines Can Crush Progress". Originally published October 31, 2016
- Chapter 5: Failure Can Be Success
  - Adapted from the *Inc.* column "How Oprah Conquered Her Biggest Failure (and How You Can, Too". Originally published August 15, 2017
- Chapter 6: Do Good Enough
  - Adapted from the *Inc.* column "Why Good Enough is the Best Path to Serious Success". Originally published February 9, 2017

- - Paulo Coelho quote: Oprah's Super Soul Conversations podcast, "Paulo Coelho, Part 1: What If the Universe Conspired in Your Favor?". Originally aired August 9, 2017.
- Chapter 7: Know Your Sacrifice
  - Adapted from the *Inc.* column "Seth Godin's Secret to Success is Quitting – and So Is Yours". Originally published March 7, 2017
- Chapter 8: The Ultimate Time Limit
  - Adapted from the *Inc.* column "Why Death is the Secret to Your Personal Success". Originally published March 23, 2017

- II: Take In:
  - Opening quote: Bryan Tracy, *How to Start and Succeed in Your Own Business* (Nightingale-Conant 2014)
- Chapter 11: Carry One Thing at a Time
  - Thich Nhat Hanh quote: *The Lion's Roar*, "The Moment is Perfect". Originally published May 1, 2008.
- Chapter 12: Build Like You're Already There
  - Adapted from the *Inc.* column "Tony Robbins' Mentor on How to Build Success Now". Originally published June 8, 2017

- Chapter 13: The 20/20 Technique
    - Adapted from the *Inc.* column "How to Prevent Others from Wasting Your Time". Originally published September 19, 2017
- Chapter 14: Theory is Just That
    - Adapted from the *Inc.* column "The Best Mike Tyson Quote on Emotional Intelligence". Originally published April 11, 2017
- Chapter 15: Doing Their Best
    - Adapted from the *Inc.* column "Brene Brown on the 1 Question You Need to Ask About People You Truly Dislike". Originally published March 16, 2017

- Chapter 16: It Isn't Your Money
    - Adapted from the *Inc.* column "A Millionaire Entrepreneur Shares How to Be Happy (and It's Not by Making Lots of Money)". Originally published December 19, 2016
- Chapter 17: Why You Are More Successful Than You Think
    - Adapted from the *Inc.* column "A Millionaire Entrepreneur Shares How to Be Happy (and It's Not by Making Lots of Money)". Originally published December 5, 2016

Acknowledgments

Writing THE BITE-SIZED ENTREPRENEUR trilogy has been a wonderful, challenging road! There are countless people who have been supportive along the way.

Thanks to the feedback and support from Randy Dotinga, Evelyn Kane, Chia Hwu, Atul Techchandani, Monique Woodard, David Goldenberg, Christina Brodbeck, Mihad Ali, and Mark McGuire, and my editor/goal-buddy/friend Jeanette Hurt and cover artist Bec Loss. Love and respect to my past and present partners, including my Cuddlr co-founder Charlie Williams, as well as my insightful colleagues in the publishing industry, particularly Marilyn Allen and Chris Barsanti. A special blessing to my partnerships that ended poorly; thank you for the lessons.

Articulating the transition from journalist to entrepreneur would have been much more difficult without great sounding boards like E. B. Boyd, Peter Economy, Minda Zetlin, Justin Bariso, Andrea King Collier, Randy Dotinga, A. Raymond Johnson, and Stephan Garnett.

A big hat-tip to Steven Pressfield, Brene Brown, Pema Chodron, Mihaly Csikszentmihalyi, Peter Sims, Mark Suster, Seth Godin, Caroline Myss, Jim Rohn, Jason Fried, David Heinemeier Hansson, and Alan Weiss. I hope to make even a shred of the significant impact you have made on the many artists, dreamers, and creators.

Love and respect to Kayt Sukel, Jenny Blake, Nilofer Merchant, Srinivas Rao, Laura Vanderkam, Cameron Herold, Kelly K. James, Scott Steinberg, Meagan Francis, Priest Willis, Jeffrey Shaw, Candice Matthews, and Leida Snow. I appreciate your wisdom, camaraderie, and friendship.

Special thanks to *Inc. Magazine*'s Laura Lorber, Douglas Cantor, and Kevin Ryan for supporting the growth of our Sane Success column that inspired this book series. IDG's Jim Malone and Jennifer Dionne, *UNUM*'s Brian Jacob Baker, *Four Seasons Magazine*'s Alicia Miller, Ellis Harman, and Waynette Goodson, *The Costco Connections*' Steve Fisher, and *Entertainment Tonight*'s Shana Krochmal were priceless allies, too.

Lastly, respect to my entrepreneurial parents Bernadette Johnson, David Brown, and Tony Howard, my brother, A. Raymond Johnson, my sisters Deirdra Bishop and Toni Howard, and my wife, Dr. Parul Patel, as well as our precocious boys Alec and Abhi. I love you.

ABOUT THE AUTHOR

Damon Brown is a long-time journalist and author of several books, most notably *Our Virtual Shadow: Why We Are Obsessed with Documenting Our Lives Online* (TED Books 2013) and *Porn & Pong: How Grand Theft Auto, Tomb Raider and Other Sexy Games Changed Our Culture* (Feral House 2008), as well as the coffeetable book *Playboy's Greatest Covers* (Sterling Publishing 2012). THE BALANCED BITE-SIZED ENTREPRENEUR is his 20th book and the third in the best-selling THE BITE-SIZED ENTREPRENEUR trilogy.

Damon co-founded the social meetup app Cuddlr while being the primary caretaker to his infant. It went number one on the Apple App store twice, changing the cultural conversation around platonic intimacy. The app was acquired less than a year after it launched, and the whirlwind experience inspired Damon's popular *Inc.com* column Sane Success as well as THE BITE-SIZED ENTREPRENEUR.

You can catch Damon in *Playboy*, *Fast Company*, and *Entrepreneur*, as well as at any locale that serves really spicy food. He lives in Toledo, Ohio, with his wife, two young sons, and bottles of hot sauce.

Connect with him at www.damonbrown.net or on Twitter at @browndamon.